How Will I Get Through the Holidays?

12 Ideas for Those Whose Loved One Has Died

James E. Miller

Willowgreen Publishing

To Christy,
so full of life, so full of love

Several people generously offered their assistance in creating this book. Ray Deabel, Delores Bastian, and Lee Battey offered helpful input. Jean Cleary, Jennifer Levine, and Donna O'Toole made time-consuming editorial suggestions. Clare Barton handled administrative details too numerous to recount. And Bernie Miller was always present, reacting to ideas, responding to changes, and generally redeeming the day.

Willowgreen Publishing
10351 Dawson's Creek Blvd., Suite B
Fort Wayne, Indiana 46825-1904
260-490-2222

Library of Congress Catalogue
Card Number: 95-91007

ISBN 978-1-885933-22-5

The yule-log sparkled keen with frost,
No wing of wind the region swept,
But over all things brooding slept
The quiet sense of something lost.

ALFRED, LORD TENNYSON
(Written after the death of his best friend
just before the holidays, 1833)

The holiest of all holidays are those
Kept by ourselves in silence and apart;
The secret anniversaries of the heart.

HENRY WADSWORTH LONGFELLOW

Whatever your age, whoever has died, whatever the cause of death, holidays lived in the absence of someone dear can be very difficult times. Customary routines are ended, never to be repeated in quite the same way. Easy-going laughter, once so natural, may become awkward or even altogether missing. Gift-giving, once so filled with fun, may seem somehow empty and sad. Familiar songs, once so comforting, may catch in your throat or bring tears to your eyes.

All this happens against a backdrop of significant questions you may find yourself asking: What exactly is happening to me? Can I possibly survive this, and do I even want to? How long will this turmoil last? Is what I am feeling normal? Am I losing touch with my sanity?

The holiday period itself adds its own share of questions: How can I make it through all the events of the holidays while missing so desperately the one I love? Would I be better off to ignore the holidays this year? Should I act as if everything were normal? Should I make major changes in my holiday rituals?

If you're like most people in grief, you will have many questions. It's important for you to know at the outset there are few universal "right" and "wrong" answers. There may be *various* answers, depending upon the unique factors of your situation: who you are as a person, what your family is like, who it was who died, when and how they died, what your relationship with that person

The eager fate which carried thee
Took the largest part of me:
For this losing is true dying.

RALPH WALDO EMERSON

*Y*et we have gone on living,
Living and partly living.

T. S. ELIOT

was, and the role that person played in your holiday rituals, to name only a few. It's also important to remember that not all your questions will have ready answers. Sometimes you must learn by doing, and then learn even better by trying it another way.

Keeping in mind there has never been a loss precisely like yours, there are still some general guidelines bereaved people have found helpful through the years. I will propose twelve of them. I hope you will treat them as suggestions rather than as prescriptions. Use them as ideas you can expand upon. Shape them to fit your distinct circumstances and to serve your personal needs. Above all else, remember that others, many others, have faced something similar to what you're facing right now. They have learned what it is like to endure and to survive and often even to grow through their experience. What they have learned is what you can learn, too. The ways they have persevered are ways you can adopt as well.

Most of all, I hope you'll choose to believe this: your holidays can still be a significant time for you. They will be different, but they can still be meaningful. They may hurt, but they can also hold hope—even great hope.

Jim Miller

There is no despair so absolute
as that which comes from the first moments
of our first great sorrow,
when we have not yet known
what it is to have suffered and be healed,
to have despaired and recovered hope.

GEORGE ELIOT (MARY ANN EVANS)

~ 1 ~
Accept the likelihood of your pain.

When you're facing your first holiday without the one who has been so close to you, a good starting point is with this awareness: chances are it will be a painful time. You may wonder how you will ever make it through.

This may or may not comfort you, but it is true: your pain is a sign you have been blessed to draw very close to another. You have loved and you have been loved. The hurt you feel is an indication of your wonderful humanness, your sensitivity, your openness. It is a proof that another has touched you deeply, even as you have touched them. While you may wish you did not hurt as much as you do, you dare not forget that your pain is none other than the result of your joy.

Even so, you may feel you would like to bypass the entire holiday period and not participate in it at all. That's a common response. During the final two months of the calendar year, however, holiday reminders are visible almost everywhere you look and audible in almost everything you hear. It's impossible to avoid the impact of this season. The energy you would spend evading what is going on all around you will be more creatively spent adapting to the reality of what this particular season holds for you.

Similarly, it is probably unwise to pretend everything is perfectly normal, and that this year's festivities will be no different than any other year's. The death of this important person in your life has created a conspicuous void. You may feel that, of course, any time of the year. But this is especially the case during the

*To come to the pleasure you have not
you must go by a way in which you enjoy not.
To come to the knowledge you have not
you must go by a way in which you know not.
To come to the possession you have not
you must go by a way in which you possess not.
To come to be where you are not
you must go by a way in which you are not.*

John of the Cross

holidays. You expect to include those you love in your holiday celebrations—with the cards you write, the gifts you give, the meals you share, the rituals you re-enact. The one who has died, however, cannot be included, at least in the way you wish. And you're reminded of this time after time in the way families are portrayed on television, in the way loved ones are referred to in holiday songs, in the idealistic images everyone carries inside about these special times.

Remember this: few holidays are as picture-perfect as we'd like to believe. It may help to admit that from the start.

It is equally important not to decide in advance that the approaching holidays will necessarily be horrendous. While it may have its difficult moments, the approaching holiday time does not have to be an absolute catastrophe. More often than not, people report that the experience itself did not turn out to be as trying as they feared. Chances are good that can be your experience, too. Yes, you will probably feel pain. Yes, you may wish this year's calendar would skip over November and December. But, no, it does not have to be awful. There are things you can do to help.

11

*But what am I?
An infant crying in the night:
An infant crying for the light:
And with no language but a cry.*

ALFRED, LORD TENNYSON

~ 2 ~

Feel whatever it is you feel.

You may be learning what many others have learned: some people will try to hurry you through your grief. Some may insist on continually cheering you up. Others may give you advice about what you should and shouldn't do or about how you should and shouldn't feel.

Whatever else you do this holiday time, do your best to claim your own feelings. As much as you are able, own up to the fact that something terribly important has happened in your life, that this naturally causes a reaction within you. You're not a robot—you're a responsive human being who is capable of all sorts of emotions.

No one else will feel what you do, in the same way, at the same time, with the same intensity. But some of the general feelings people in your situation often report include these:

• *Sadness.* It's sad to think about what you've lost, what can never happen again, what you'll have to learn to live without. It's doubly sad to experience this at such a happy time of the year.

• *Depression.* More than feeling glum, you may feel desolate or despairing. You may feel depleted of all energy, listless and alone. You may doubt you'll ever feel any better.

• *Anxiety.* You may feel nervous and jittery, ill at ease and full of uncertainty.

• *Fear.* You may be afraid of what will happen to you, how you'll cope, what you'll do, even if you'll survive.

• *Anger.* Being mad is a common response—mad at people

*Better to be without logic
than without feeling.*

CHARLOTTE BRONTE

*One day – an idea that will horrify you now –
this intolerable misfortune will become
a blessed memory of a being
who will never again leave you.
But you are in a stage of unhappiness
where it is impossible for you to have faith
in these reassurances.*

MARCEL PROUST
From a letter to a recently bereaved friend

who don't understand you or support you, angry about how the death happened and who was involved, even provoked at the person who died. You may be upset with yourself, or with God, or with the whole world.

• *Guilt.* You may dwell upon what you did or didn't do while the other person was alive. You may feel guilty you're living and the other is not, or that you have moments of happiness in the midst of your grief.

• *Apathy.* You may find that you experience almost no feelings at all. You may feel numb and impassive. Or you may feel confused and disoriented.

There are many other feelings, of course: relief, respect, pride, joy, compassion, and love all come to mind as well. Whatever it is you're feeling these days, remind yourself that feelings are normal, whatever they happen to be. They're a sign that you're human, that you care deeply, and that whatever you feel today, you can feel differently tomorrow.

Your feelings seldom lead you astray. They usually lead you to yourself.

*Give sorrow words: the grief that does not speak
Whispers the o'er-fraught heart and bids it break.*

WILLIAM SHAKESPEARE

~ 3 ~
Express your emotions.

Acknowledging your feelings to yourself is one step, but another step is just as important: you must find a release for what is going on inside you.

There are many different ways to express yourself. Search for what works best for you. Some cry long and hard, and others cry hardly at all. People are different that way. Some prefer to talk a lot, and others tend to be more quiet. Some like to write, while others keep their hands busy in different ways. The secret for your best means of expression is simple: be yourself.

Many people find real value in speaking their feelings to family members and closest friends, while others are comfortable with acquaintances, colleagues, and even people they barely know. The important thing is to choose someone who will listen, especially someone who listens well and responds thoughtfully. Sometimes a person who has known their own serious losses can be with you in a way others cannot. A grief support group can also be a healthy choice for someone in your situation.

You may be one who turns more easily to the written word. If you have not been a journal keeper, now is a good time to begin. Regular journaling helps get feelings off your chest, it helps clarify your thinking, and it helps you monitor your progress through grief. If you wish, you can write letters to the one who died. You can compose stories and fashion poems. You can record your dreams and look for their subtle messages. You can preserve your wonderings and expand on your ponderings.

One often calms one's grief by recounting it.

PIERRE CORNEILLE

I have something more to do than to feel.

CHARLES LAMB
From a letter just after his mother died

*Blessed are those who mourn,
for they shall be comforted.*

JESUS OF NAZARETH

Some people best express their feelings with music—by singing or playing an instrument. Others like to pray their feelings, or express them through body movement.

It is also possible for you to convey your emotions in more tangible ways. People have been known to give expression to their innermost selves by creating something out of wood, molding something out of clay, quilting something out of cloth, or painting something on canvas. The possibilities are almost limitless.

Whatever method you choose, find a way to allow your feelings to move from within yourself to outside yourself. You'll feel better. You'll learn more. You'll gain perspective. And you'll be placing yourself squarely on the path that leads toward healing.

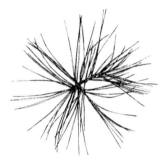

*When schemes are laid in advance,
it is surprising how often the circumstances
fit in with them.*

SIR WILLIAM OSLER

~ 4 ~
Plan ahead.

Perhaps the most practical advice is this: plan your day before it arrives. Realizing that this year's holidays, and maybe several years' holidays, will not unfold the way you'd wish, you can make plans to do the best you can with the circumstances you face. You can prepare yourself to deal with what you think will be the more difficult situations. You can give thought to how you will cope with those parts of your celebration that are especially emotion-laden, or how you will handle those tasks or roles that were the special responsibility of your loved one. You can ask others to help you, both in thinking about what you'll do and in carrying out your ideas.

Talk things over with the people with whom you traditionally share the holidays. Among the issues that might be discussed are these: What is it about the approaching holidays that most concerns you? What do you need for others to understand about you during this time? What can other people do to help you? What can they refrain from doing? What can you do to help others? What are some creative ways you might handle the holiday celebrations so you can be true to the spirit of the season while being honest about the loss you have suffered? You will probably find that open conversation and brainstorming of thoughts will give you some positive ideas. Make sure you listen to people of all ages, including the young.

After a painful death, one family brought novelty to their celebration by introducing a different country's theme each year—

*It is a mistake to look too far ahead.
Only one link in the chain of destiny
can be handled at a time.*

SIR WINSTON CHURCHILL

*People have to learn sometimes
not only how much the heart,
but how much the head,
can bear.*

MARIA MITCHELL

a Spanish holiday fiesta one time, a Swedish observance the next. Another family decided to add more structure to their time together by playing a round-robin tournament of a favorite game all afternoon. You might elect to go to a movie, or bring one in. You might invite someone new to your celebration or even a whole group of people. You might elect to join another family's festivities if that feels right.

Give thought to the various choices you might make, knowing that choices are available. Try listing your options on paper to help clarify your thinking.

Consider doing something similar with the many tasks you face as you prepare for this time, finding ways to divide them into smaller, more manageable units. Slowly, you will probably find that you are able to do what you feel is best.

When planning ahead, make decisions for the immediate holiday period only. You don't need to decide about the years ahead. And whatever you do, plan tentatively. You haven't been through this particular holiday while experiencing this particular loss. Give yourself the freedom to change your plans as you go. You deserve that leeway.

It *is for us to pray*
not for tasks equal to our powers,
but for powers equal to our tasks,
to go forward with a great desire
forever beating at the door of our hearts
as we travel towards our distant goal.

HELEN KELLER

~ 5 ~
Take charge where you can.

There is much in your life, of course, that has moved beyond your command. The loss you've experienced and the resulting inescapable changes have robbed you of a power you may have taken for granted. Yet there are some actions you can take and some decisions you can make that are within your authority. Begin to take control of your life in specific ways, even if those ways seem small.

If the death you've experienced isn't too recent, this may be a good time to evaluate the holiday traditions you've established through the years. Which ones are meaningful, ones you want to keep? Which ones have outgrown their usefulness? Which ones might you forego for a year or two, and which ones are so important to you that you must perform them, even if it's hard to do? Which ones can you adapt to fit this year's circumstances?

Generally speaking, this is usually not the best time to make drastic changes, like starting life over in a new town, or celebrating the holidays in a faraway place among people who do not appreciate what has happened to you. But some changes can be healthy and even important to make. It might make sense to change your holiday meal routine, by dining out at a restaurant rather than at home, or by having the main meal in another's home, or by planning a new menu. Changes might be made in how holiday decorations are done. Or how gifts are given out, or when, or where. Consider designing new rituals—ones that will include opportunities to remember the past while acknowledging that the

Step by step the ladder is ascended.

GEORGE HERBERT

Sometimes, I think, the things we see
Are shadows of the things to be,
That what we plan we build.

PHOEBE CARY

present has changed.

Keep in mind there are other ways for you to assume some control over your life. Eating healthfully and drinking wisely is a good start. Maintain your exercise program, or begin one if you've not been in the habit. Research has demonstrated this will help you feel better, mentally as well as physically. A brisk walk each day is one of the best exercises you can perform, especially if you can do it out of doors. Consult your physician if you have any questions.

Another action you can take is to try to get your proper amount of sleep. Go to bed early enough to get the rest you need. If you're sleeping too much, limit your time in bed. It's not unusual, however, for your sleep patterns to change for awhile, even a long while.

In general, choose life in all the ways you can. Be among people who offer you vitality. Practice those disciplines that bring you energy. Do those things that give you satisfaction. Take charge in little ways and you'll find they're not so little—they're very important.

What is a friend?
A single soul in two bodies.

ARISTOTLE

I felt it shelter to speak to you.

EMILY DICKINSON

~ 6 ~
Turn to others for support.

The holiday time, when emotions naturally run high and memories are especially strong, is a difficult time to be entirely alone. People who are bereaved can benefit greatly from the support and assistance of people who understand and care. Don't forget that often these people not only want to help, but they need to help. For that is one way they can work through their own feelings—for the person who has died, for you and your loss, and for their own reactions toward death and grief in general. In other words, by allowing others to help you, you can help them.

There was a time when mourning practices were clear, including what you were to do as a bereaved person and what others were to do in supporting you. That's no longer the case. Sadly, many people today have little idea what people like you most need. You may have to let them know in all kindness how they can help, and then allow them to do so.

Try to be understanding of those who are hesitant to express their caring, afraid they will "upset" you or "say the wrong thing." Such people are usually feeling very uncomfortable, and in not owning up to their emotions, they create a distance between themselves and the person who longs for meaningful communication—a person like you.

Be straightforward about what you think will assist you and what won't. Express your wishes, even if it's only to one other person. Word has a way of traveling. If it feels affirming to hear your friends speak the name of your loved one, let them know. If

*To know someone here and there
whom we accord with,
who is living on with us, even in the silence –
this makes our earthly ball a peopled garden.*

JOHANN WOLFGANG VON GOETHE

*Two may talk together under the same roof
for many years, yet never really meet;
and two others at first speech are old friends.*

MARY CATHERWOOD

hugs feel good, say so. Or show it by hugging others first.

There are many ways you can be with others and others can be with you. Talking, of course, is one way. You may find that you tend to talk more than usual, and you may even repeat the same stories. That's quite normal.

Go shopping together. Attend religious services or holiday commemorations as a twosome or as a group. Go to dinner, perhaps to restaurants you wouldn't normally choose. Share books and discuss them. Go to a movie or play or sporting event and make time to talk afterwards. Visit a place you've never been. Invite people over for an evening and uncomplicate your life by serving carry-out food. Or if cooking for another is something you miss, prepare a feast. Or don't eat at all—just allow your guests to help you decorate your home for the holidays, if that is what you wish.

If you are unsure about the resources for bereaved people in your area, contact the nearest hospice. Or call the social service department of the nearest hospital. Or be in touch with your local mental health center. Many communities have a twenty-four hour crisis line for people to call. If you think you might use that service, look up the telephone number and keep it handy. You might make an appointment to speak with a rabbi, priest, or minister, or with a grief counselor. Just one or two sessions may do wonders for you.

Have patience with all the world,
but first of all with yourself.

FRANCIS DE SALES

~ 7 ~
Be gentle with yourself.

One of the best things you can do is treat yourself lovingly. The holiday season has stresses and demands all its own. Add the extreme strain bereavement may cause and overload easily becomes a problem.

Give yourself plenty of time to rest. Avoid committing yourself to doing more than you have the physical and psychological energy to handle. Accept invitations that feel right and kindly decline those that don't. Let people know that just because you choose to forgo their offer today doesn't mean you'll do the same next time. Pace yourself on your "good" days and do what feels right. Give yourself lots of latitude on your "bad" days and accept that most people in grief have their full share of these times. You're like anyone else in this situation. There's no reason to feel guilty about having such days. They simply go with the territory. And the territory is grief.

Offer yourself the time you need and the kind of time you deserve. You may desire more stretches of solitude than usual—that's often the case. Use it in ways that feel relaxing for you, whether that means reading a spiritual classic, engaging in your favorite hobby, or dozing in front of the TV. Carve out time each day and every week to do what feels refreshing to you—exploring the out of doors, doing something active and invigorating, feeding and watching the birds or squirrels, taking long baths, savoring a special treat.

Give yourself permission to ease the holiday demands that face

A deep distress hath humanized my soul.

WILLIAM WORDSWORTH

*It is only people who possess firmness
who can possess true gentleness.*

FRANCOIS LA ROCHEFOUCALD

you. If you'd rather, shop from catalogues instead of in congested malls. Or beat the holiday rush and shop early and quickly. Ask someone to shop with you for moral support, or allow them to shop for you. This may even be a year when you forgo shopping altogether.

Set easy-to-attain goals for yourself and congratulate yourself each time you achieve one. Be forgiving of yourself when you don't. Remember: you are a beginner in this process. Success takes time. You'll learn.

What the heart once owned and had,
it shall never lose.

Henry Ward Beecher

Only stay quiet while my mind remembers
The beauty of fire from the beauty of embers.

John Masefield

~ 8 ~

Remember to remember.

You may feel comfort in finding specific ways to link yourself with the one who died. One man began carrying a smooth stone in his pocket that he would quietly hold when he wanted, a ready reminder of his love for his deceased son. Another found solace in carrying a small cross. One woman wore a necklace that had belonged to her mother, while another woman, a writer, began using her father's favorite pen after he died. If you wish to use a linking object, you might select something that belonged to your loved one, or something that was made or given by her or him. You might carry it, wear it, use it, or place it in easy sight.

Some people create a small remembrance area in their home. It is often a table top or mantle, where a framed photograph or two might be placed and a few mementos arranged. A candle might be included, ready to be lit at certain times or for an entire day. Sometimes additional objects are placed nearby, representing others who have died and telling the universal story of life and death.

You might choose to honor your loved one with a ritual of remembrance. Talking about your life together or looking at photographs or home movies may be a bittersweet experience. But those same memories you hesitate to activate can also carry feelings of fondness and recollections of joy. Remembering your loved one is a way of insuring that the past does not remain only in the past. It lives on still, in you and in others.

These observances may be enacted simply and quietly, by

*Some memories are realities,
and are better than anything
that can ever happen to one again.*

WILLA CATHER

*Yet if you should forget me for a while
And afterwards remember, do not grieve:
Better by far you should forget and smile
Than that you should remember and be sad.*

CHRISTINA ROSSETTI

remembering the deceased in a prayer, for example, or with a toast before dinner, or by lighting a small taper that burns as you eat. Other rituals may become more involved. You may symbolically remember the other's life with a planned ceremony in your home, or with a round of storytelling that makes that person's essence come alive again. You might plant a special tree for them, either at home or somewhere else.

One woman buys her deceased husband a cow each year—she makes a donation to the Heifer Project, his favorite charity. You might do something similar, donating the same amount of money you would have spent on your loved one's gifts. Another woman placed a Christmas tree on her husband's grave, which she and her small children decorated lovingly.

Many congregations, hospices, and hospitals host meaningful ceremonies of remembrance at the holidays. So do certain funeral homes. Some cities host community-wide events to help the newly bereaved prepare for their first holidays alone. Look around for what's available in your area.

One final point about remembering to remember is this: you may not feel up to it this year. That's not uncommon for someone new to grief. If that's the case for you, don't force yourself. You'll know when the time is right.

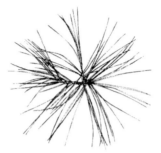

Amid my list of blessings infinite,
Stands this the foremost,
"That my heart has bled."

EDWARD YOUNG

~ 9 ~
Search out and count your blessings.

Remain as open as you are able to what you have to appreciate and to what may be given you during the coming holiday season. While you may regularly feel sad or listless or alone, you don't have to be limited to only those feelings. You have other possibilities as well.

You may find a quiet happiness in how young people can bring real life to the holidays with their innocent expectation and their exuberant joy. You may discover a profound closeness with others, an intimacy you have not known in quite the same way before, for it grows out of the way your life has been torn open. You may come upon moments of serendipity when you least expect them, when the holiday spirit becomes real in a way you could not have predicted.

During what may seem like an impossible holiday period, much is possible. You may find an assuring richness to your times of solitude. You may surprise yourself with how meaningful and instructive your journaling time becomes. You may come to realize that your faith is stronger than you imagined, or that it's growing deeper in ways you would not have thought. You may find comfort in familiar words that take on a new force. You may make some unforgettable discoveries—about yourself, about your relationship with your loved one, about life as a whole—as you take time to absorb the lessons of creation all around you, or as you meditate quietly, or as you read reflectively.

Accept my thoughts for thanks;
I have no words.

HANNAH MORE

O world, I cannot hold thee close enough!

EDNA ST. VINCENT MILLAY

In time you may begin to discover what so many have discovered before you—that your grief experience is leading you, however slowly and however tentatively, to begin to change and to grow. You may realize you are becoming a different person, a more mature one. Hard as it may be to understand, you may begin to see that in giving yourself over to your hurt, you are beginning to heal. And in the act of losing, you are somehow aware there is something you will gain.

One secret to handling the holidays is to stay in the present moment as much as possible. Savor what there is to savor, however small. Accept the warmth that is yours to receive, however fleeting. Cry if tears are near, then let them pass and see what else you will feel. And don't be afraid to laugh. There can be humor both in what you remember and in the events of these passing days themselves. Enjoy any laughter that flows. You won't be desecrating the memory of your loved one. You'll be consecrating what he or she has brought to your life, and you'll be doing your own mending at the same time.

All that is not given is lost.

INDIAN PROVERB

A woman or man with outward courage
dares to die.
A man or woman with inward courage
dares to live.

LAO TZU

~ 10 ~
Do something for others.

It only makes sense that people in grief can become centered on themselves. Their loss feels so overwhelming and the tasks facing them seem so demanding, they may focus their attention almost exclusively on what has happened and how it affects them. Perhaps you have experienced that yourself. Early in the grief process, such a response is to be expected. Yet after awhile it is helpful to place some of your attention outside yourself. One way of doing that is by doing something for others.

Even if your needs are many, yours are not the only needs. And even if your grief weighs you down, you do not have to remain incapacitated by your loss. You can reach out and offer something of what you have and who you are, even if it feels like it's only a little. Chances are you'll make a couple of discoveries. You'll learn that what you have to offer can mean a great deal to someone else. And you'll probably find that you have more and more to offer as you go along.

There are so many possibilities. You can take care of someone's child or their pet, for a few hours or a few days. You can cook meals, volunteer at food pantries, sew cancer pads, check on shut-ins, assist in hospitals or nursing homes. You can drive, shovel, telephone, mow, clean, trim, deliver, type, greet, and perform countless other acts, depending upon your interests and your abilities. Do what you feel comfortable doing and what brings meaning to your days and to others' lives.

One man volunteered his Christmas Eve beside the bed of a

*The one who wishes to secure the good of others
has already secured one's own.*

CONFUCIUS

*We do not love people so much
for the good they have done to us,
as for the good we have done them.*

LEO TOLSTOY

hospitalized child so the parents could spend the evening at home with their other children who needed them. It was hard to tell who was more gratified.

If you're unsure how to reach out, contact the volunteer department of a nearby hospital or nursing home. Perhaps there's something you can do for organizations like the League for the Blind, the Cancer Society, the Red Cross, or Big Brothers/Big Sisters. If your community doesn't have a volunteer service bureau, try contacting your local United Way agency or look under "social service organizations" in the yellow pages.

Much can happen when you reach out to others. You'll be drawn out of your own life and into other people's lives. You'll be touched by the simple wisdom of children, or by the interesting stories of other families, or by the inspirational ways others have coped with unwanted events in their lives.

Such giving of yourself may offer other rewards. It may help you place your personal loss in a broader perspective. You'll have the opportunity to feel needed and appreciated and valued. Certainly you'll help others, and you'll be doing something positive for yourself at the same time. In fact, you may feel that you're benefiting more than anyone. If that's the case, just smile your knowing smile and keep on doing what feels good.

Where there is sorrow there is holy ground.

OSCAR WILDE

There is more faith in honest doubt,
Believe me, than in half the creeds.

ALFRED, LORD TENNYSON

~ 11 ~
Give voice to your soul.

A time of grief is a time for your soul. Anytime you suffer a serious loss, the spiritual side of you will be a part of whatever happens. You may not use words like "soul" or "spirit." You may not refer to the vocabulary or the beliefs of a particular faith. But some inner part of you is still involved, a part that is other than your body or your mind or your feelings.

You may be one whose faith is obvious in your life. You may turn naturally to the resources of your religious experience and find there a foundation that anchors you. Assurances and explanations from the ages may calm your fears and enrich your understanding. You may discover how supportive and nurturing your community of faith can be.

Whatever your religious background and whatever your spiritual inclinations, you may find yourself asking serious questions like these: How could God let this happen? Is there even a God at all, given what has occurred? How do I fit this loss into my belief system?

Some people become very upset with God. Some develop doubts they've never had before. Some feel shaken and lost, unsure of their foundations.

You can keep several things in mind if your spirit is troubled. A large number of people ask similar questions and face similar doubts at a time like this. You're not alone. Be aware also that these same questions and doubts are voiced in the official texts of most major religions—they're not new to you, nor are they neces-

49

Nothing before, nothing behind;
The steps of faith
Fall on the seeming void, and find
The rock beneath.

JOHN GREENLEAF WHITTIER

If thou wishest to search out
the deep things of God,
search out the depths
of thine own spirit.

RICHARD OF SAINT-VICTOR

sarily unreligous. If anything, they are a sign you take these spiritual matters very seriously. Remember too that what you wonder about or what you believe today is not the final word. You're on a journey, one of the most difficult and important journeys of your life. Where you are today is not where you'll end up tomorrow.

Consider making some room in your days for the expression of your soul. Depending upon what feels natural, this might mean times of prayer, or quiet meditation, or reading spiritual books, or talking with a religious professional. Learn how others have responded when their crisis of grief and crisis of faith occurred simultaneously.

The death you have experienced has exposed you to new realities of living and to new possibilities about what life and death, meaning and purpose are all about. Go deeper. See what answers await you in the wisdom of the ages, in talks with close friends and trusted confidants, in silent walks through forests and beside waters and atop mountains.

And realize that the answers you seek may not be mysteriously hidden far way. They may be waiting for you patiently, deep inside. You don't need to chase after them. All you need do is sit still.

Let me not pray to be sheltered from dangers
but to be fearless in facing them.
Let me not beg for the stilling of my pain
but for the heart to conquer it.

RABINDRANATH TAGORE

~ 12 ~
Harbor hope.

You may wish your awful pain would go away. You may be tired of feeling tired, or depressed about your ongoing depression. You may wonder if your grief will ever end, if life will ever return with the zest you once knew.

Good news awaits you. Almost all people who undergo the major kind of loss you are experiencing recover their original interest in life again. It takes time, but it happens. It takes effort, but it unfolds. There are those who become even more in touch with life than they were before. Their moments grow richer. Their understanding grows fuller. Their love grows deeper.

No one likes to grieve. Yet it is the very act of grieving that leads you back to life. It is only by allowing yourself to feel bad that you can finally come to feel good again. But until that feeling recurs, what can you do? Among other things, you can hope.

You can hope that by staying open to the demands of this experience, you will be enlarged as a person, and by grappling with the fullness of your feelings, you will be strengthened as a human being.

You can hope that this experience of separation will draw you closer to others, and that your relationship with the one who died will change form without changing focus, allowing you to feel connected while still being apart.

You can hope that you will integrate this loss into your life, so that you're growing wiser as well as older, and so that you're more prepared to face those other losses in your life which will inevitably

If winter comes, can spring be far behind?

PERCY BYSSHE SHELLEY

The lowest ebb is the turn of the tide.

HENRY WADSWORTH LONGFELLOW

follow.

You can hope that others will be there for you when you need them most, and if they are not, you can hope you will find the companionship you need within. You can hope that when you feel most alone, you sense that you are not completely alone, that you are held by Another who will not let you go.

You can hope that when you need to endure, perseverance will be yours. That when you need to attempt what you haven't tried before, both ingenuity and courage will be present in equal measure. That when you need to believe because knowledge can go no further, faith will be there to escort you.

There is one more thing you can hope for. If you find that hope eludes you and the future stretches before you dark and bleak, then you can ask another person to hold your hope for you, and to believe in you even when you have difficulty believing in yourself. Then their hope can sustain your hope.

Never forget that this is one of the most powerful tools you have. With hope, you can heal. With hope, you can venture forward. With hope, you can be yourself again. And with hope, you can find a way to carry with you the one you so miss and the one you so love.

You have had many and great sadnesses.
But, please, consider whether these great sadnesses
have not gone right to the center of yourself?
Whether much in you has not altered,
whether you have not somewhere,
at some point of your being,
undergone a change while you were sad?
For our sadnesses are the moments when something new
has entered into us, something unknown;
our feelings grow mute in the perplexity,
everything in us withdraws, a stillness comes,
and the new, which no one knows,
stands in the midst of it
and is silent.

RAINER MARIA RILKE

A Final Word of Promise

It is, of course, difficult to grieve anytime. It is doubly difficult during those times when your thoughts turn so tenderly to the one who was such an important part of the past, the one whose absence is felt so painfully in the present. This is true of holidays as it is of other special days: birthdays and anniversaries, Mother's Day and Father's Day, Valentine's Day and vacation days—any days you and your loved one made dear.

The task before you may seem huge. Some days it will take as much effort as you can muster. Other days it may ask of you more than you think you have to give.

You will need to be strong in your determination. But you'll only need to do that one single minute or one individual hour at a time. And for those times when your determination wanes, you can forgive yourself and begin again when you are able.

You will need to be flexible in how you approach your holiday celebrations, but you won't have to know exactly how to do that. You can learn as you go, and you can have others beside you who are learning to be flexible with you.

You will need to accept the rise and fall of your feelings and to understand that your emotions will have a life of their own. But you need not worry about these fluctuations. Almost all bereaved people experience them. They are nature's way of helping you adjust gradually and safely to the loss you have suffered.

You will probably need to search for meaning in what has happened to you and your loved one, but you do not have to go alone in that search. Others have made the journey before you and they have left markers all along the way. Still others are making a

Death is not putting out the light.
It is only extinguishing a lamp
because the day has come.

RABINDRANATH TAGORE

I do not seek to understand so that I can believe,
but I believe so that I may understand;
and what is more,
I believe that unless I do believe,
I shall not understand.

SAINT ANSELM

similar journey at the same time you are. It's possible to travel hand in hand.

Most likely you will need to look carefully at who you are as an individual in light of what has happened to you. This is an appropriate time for you to ask not just "What have I lost?" but also "What have I kept?", "What will I never lose?", and "How am I growing?". You can choose to believe that one day you will have an answer for this question: "What have I gained?".

If you wish to experience growth through your grief, you will do well to open yourself to at least one other person, and perhaps several other people. For others can often see what you cannot see. They can sometimes do what you cannot do. And they can listen to the fullness of your story, a story that begs to be told.

If you wish for your grief to help link you with the one who has died, even after your grief has ended, then you will find value in realizing that the love you have known does not disappear when one of you stops walking the earth. Your relationship will change form and expression. But it will remain a relationship.

Finally, you can negotiate your way through this experience of grief by giving yourself love. This will best be expressed when you forgive yourself when you fall short of your expectations, by pampering yourself when you feel stretched beyond your limits, and by affirming yourself each time you take a positive step, and each time you don't.

In the unfolding of time, you are likely to discover you are being changed by your encounter with death and grief. You will no longer be the way you once were. You will be transformed. You will be more sure of what you hold dear. You will be more clear in voice, more sharp in sight, more tender in touch. You will be more

What we have once enjoyed and deeply loved
we can never lose, for all that we love deeply
becomes a part of us.

HELEN KELLER

Lay up for yourselves treasures in heaven,
where neither moth nor rust consumes
and where thieves do not break in and steal.
For where your treasure is,
there will be your heart also.

JESUS OF NAZARETH

connected with all forms of life, and more understanding of all forms of death. You will be more fully "you."

Without question, you will pay a price for your growth, a price you may not want to pay. You will have to let go of what the past was like, while you carry it with you in memory. You will have to release who you were, so you can become who you are being called to be.

The journey before you is not easy. But it is doable. And there is help all along the way—whether it comes from others who are around you or others who have gone before you, whether it's from deep within yourself or a Source far beyond yourself.

May you come to feel that your life is the richer for the experiences you've known, the love you've felt, the loss you're enduring, and the strength you're gaining. May you find it within yourself in time to be able to look back and say,

I have known many blessings in my life. I have lost, but I have also gained. I have hurt, but I have also healed. I have struggled, but I have also loved. And I have been loved. I know I still have more to experience, more to change, more to grow. For all that I have been given in ever so many ways, I know that I am blessed. And I am thankful.

Additional Resources by James E. Miller

Loss and Grief

Books

What Will Help Me?
12 Things to Remember When You Have Suffered A Loss

How Can I Help?
12 Things To Do When Someone You Know Suffers A Loss

A Pilgrimage Through Grief
Healing the Soul's Hurt After Loss

When Mourning Dawns
Living Your Way Fully Through the Seasons of Your Grief

One You Love Has Died
Ideas for How Your Grief Can Help You Heal

Videotapes & DVDs

Invincible Summer
Returning to Life After Someone You Love Has Died

Listen to Your Sadness
Finding Hope Again After Despair Invades Your Life

How Do I Go On?
Re-designing Your Future After Crisis Has Changed Your Life

By the Waters of Babylon
A Spiritual Pilgrimage for Those Who Feel Dislocated

We Will Remember
A Meditation for Those Who Live On

When Mourning Dawns: The Video/DVD

Transition and Older Age

Books

Change & Possibility
Discovering Hope in Life's Transitions

Autumn Wisdom
Finding Meaning in Life's Later Years

Videotapes & DVDs

Nothing Is Permanent Except Change
Learning to Manage Transition in Your Life

Gaining a Heart of Wisdom
Finding Meaning in the Autumn of Your Life

Illness and Caregiving

Books

This Time of Caregiving
Words of Encouragement and Hope

When You're the Caregiver
12 Things to Do If Someone You Care For Is Ill or Incapacitated

When You're Ill or Incapacitated
12 Things to Remember in Times of Sickness, Injury, or Disability

The Art of Being a Healing Presence
A Guide for Those in Caring Relationships

The Art of Listening in a Healing Way

Videotapes & DVDs

The Grit and Grace of Being a Caregiver
Maintaining Your Balance as You Care for Others

The Art of Listening in a Healing Way: The Video/DVD

James E. Miller is a writer, photographer, spiritual director, workshop leader, and speaker who creates resources and gives presentations in the areas of loss, transition, caregiving, healing presence, spirituality, and older age. He is a frequent speaker before many professional groups and at various institutions, often incorporating his own award-winning photography. He leads workshops and conducts retreats throughout North America.

To discuss bringing him to your area, call 260/490-2222 or email *jmiller@willowgreen.com*.